Wicked Whodunits

Dr. Quicksolve Mini-Mysteries

Jim Sukach

Illustrated by
Tatjana Mai-Wyss

Sterling Publishing Co., Inc.
New York

Library of Congress Cataloging-in-Publication Data

Sukach, Jim.
  Wicked whodunits / Jim Sukach ; illustrated by Tatjana Mai-Wyss.
    p. cm.
  Includes index.
  ISBN 1-4027-0400-3
  1. Puzzles. 2. Detective and mystery stories. I. Title.
GV1507.D4 S829 2002
793.73—dc21

                                        2002151751

10 9 8 7 6 5 4 3 2 1

Published in paperback in 2005 by Sterling Publishing Co., Inc.
387 Park Avenue South, New York, NY 10016
© 2003 by James Richard Sukach
Distributed in Canada by Sterling Publishing
c/o Canadian Manda Group, 165 Dufferin Street,
Toronto, Ontario, Canada M6K 3H6
Distributed in Great Britain and Europe by Chris Lloyd
at Orca Book Services, Stanley House, Fleets Lane,
Poole BH15 3AJ, England
Distributed in Australia by Capricorn Link (Australia)
Pty. Ltd., P.O. Box 704, Windsor, NSW 2756, Australia

Manufactured in the United States of America
All rights reserved

Sterling ISBN 1-4027-0400-3 Hardcover
            ISBN 1-4027-2793-3 Paperback

For information about custom editions, special sales, premium and
corporate purchases, please contact Sterling Special Sales
Department at 800-805-5489 or specialsales@sterlingpub.com.

Contents

Dr. J. L. Quicksolve   5

Now You See Him! Now You Don't!   6

Snowflakes and Signatures   9

Camping Crooks   12

Swimming Contest   16

A Cash Withdrawal   19

Seven Hills Run   21

Strike Up the Band   25

A Will and a Way   28

Campus Cop   30

Mighty Neighborly   33

Merger Murder   35

Stolen Contract   37

Winter Break   39

Sayahh.com   42

Cookie Jar Caper   45

Kidnapped Kicker   49

Another Warehouse Murder   52

Following Cecil Sapp   55

Callahan and Callahan   59

Mystery Train   63

Mystery Train Two   67

Defining Moment   73

Elliott Savant   78

The Meditators' Incident   81

Break Time   84

Answers   87

Index   96

Dr. J. L. Quicksolve

Dr. Jeffrey Lynn Quicksolve is a professor of criminology who retired early from the police department, where he earned his reputation as a brilliant detective. Now he works with various police agencies and private detectives as a consultant when he is not teaching at the university.

He certainly knows his business: solving crimes. Many people are amazed at how he solves so many crimes so quickly. He says, "The more you know about people and the world we live in, the easier it is to solve a problem."

His son Junior enjoys learning too, and he solves a few mysteries himself. Join them as they unravel mysteries. Read, listen, think carefully, and you can solve many of these crimes too!

Now You See Him! Now You Don't!

Dr. J. L. Quicksolve **had just joined** the small group of police officers in the middle of City Zoo huddled in a group like a small football team discussing strategy. There was a cool autumn breeze nipping at their cheeks. It was the "jacket weather" that Dr. Quicksolve loved. Captain Rootumout's consternation over their failure to catch their suspected diamond thief passing the goods to his accomplice added to the coolness of the moment. "Nobody saw anything?" Captain Rootumout asked.

"He was here one minute and gone the next," Sergeant Shurshot said matter-of-factly. She leaned against the long-handled broom even more matter-of-factly. It was part of her undercover costume as a zoo worker.

Officer Longarm said, "We didn't see him get close enough to anyone to pass the jewels or get any money." Officer Longarm was dressed like a large, round lady in a fur coat. No one seemed to question why he was disguised as a woman and Sergeant Shurshot was dressed like a man.

"Somebody must have seen something!" Rootumout insisted.

"If anyone can tell us anything, it might help," Dr. Quicksolve added.

"Well," said Sergeant Stratefellow, who was dressed like a mime, "there were a lot of people around."

"There was a balloon man," Officer Longarm said.

"A balloon man?" Dr. Quicksolve asked, looking around and not seeing any sign of balloons.

"That was something!" Officer Longarm said. "His balloons got away—about fifty of them! I wonder if he has to pay for them all."

"Balloons?" Dr. Quicksolve asked.

"They all went up at once," Sergeant Shurshot said. Captain Rootumout and Dr. Quicksolve looked at each other. Sergeant Shurshot caught their look and said, "I didn't see anything hooked to the balloons."

"That's an idea," Officer Longarm said. "He could have sent the diamonds up in the air so somebody could pick them up later—maybe shoot the balloons down. Should I try to find that balloon man?"

"I don't think they would have sent thousands of dollars in diamonds into the air tied to balloons," Captain Rootumout said.

"I think you're right about that, Captain, but I also think the balloon man had a role in this crime. Better check him out," Dr. Quicksolve said.

Why not use the balloons? Why check out the balloon man?

Answer on page 87.

Snowflakes
and Signatures

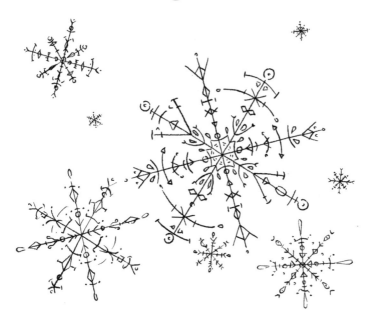

The first light snowfall of winter was just beginning when Junior's friend Skeeter raced his bicycle down the length of Junior's driveway toward the open garage where Junior sat at an old oak desk, looking intently down at some papers. Skeeter slammed on his brakes and skidded to a noisy stop. He yanked back on his handlebars, pulling the front of his bike up, and spun around in a circle on the back wheel. As he completed his spin, he yelled out, "Hi-Yo, Silver!"

Junior did not look up. "Hi, Skeeter," he mumbled down at his papers.

"What's up?" Skeeter asked.

"Well," Junior answered slowly, finally looking up, "I wasn't thinking about the Lone Ranger, but I was thinking about old movies. I was watching a Charlie Chan mystery movie last night."

"Hey, they don't show Chinese people in a very good way," Skeeter said.

"That's for sure," Junior said. "But just like cowboy and Indian shows, you can look beyond those prejudices and enjoy old films sometimes. Charlie Chan had a funny accent, and I think a real Chinese person never played him, but he was a genius at solving crimes. Nobody minds being a genius."

"That's true," Skeeter said.

"I get a lot of good ideas for solving crimes watching old detective shows like that. I've even given my dad a few good ideas."

Skeeter looked at the piles of paper on Junior's desk. About a dozen different pages had nothing on them except Junior's name. "So, what are you doing, practicing writing your signature?"

"No. That's a good idea, though. You need to decide just how you want to sign your name and do it that way all the time. It helps avoid confusion. But I was looking at something else—something from the movies. Suppose you had a question about somebody's signature—like for a will or something. You think it might be forged. So you get another signature from the original will, for example…" Junior hunted a minute and picked up one of the pages with his signature. He laid it on top of another signature and held it up toward the sunlight. "Then suppose somebody put one signature over the other, and they made a perfect match. What would that prove?"

Skeeter looked at the matching signatures, scratched his head, and said, "Well…"

What do you think?

Answer on page 87.

Camping Crooks

They arrived late at night, to set up camp in a drizzling rain. "If we hurry and get these tents set up quickly, we can avoid getting too wet," Dr. J. L. Quicksolve, the famous detective, said. He and his son, Junior, unloaded the gear. Junior's twin cousins, Flora and Fauna, spread out the two tents a few yards apart on the flattest areas they could find on their site. Lucy Looker, a friend of the family who also happened to be a famous movie actress, sorted out tent poles and laid them out along the sides of the tents where they belonged.

"Wait a minute, Flora," Dr. Quicksolve said just as Flora had begun pounding the first stake of the second tent into the ground. The twin girls were identical, and it took some time with them before anyone could tell them apart. Most people still had trouble, even their friends. "I want to turn the tent a little bit," Dr. Quicksolve said, bending down to drag the tent around to a slightly different spot. He stood up and said, "There. That's better."

The trees provided a nice canopy over their campsite. They held the dampness of the drizzle off just long enough for them to stay dry until they were finished and snug in their tents.

Junior climbed into his sleeping bag next to his dad who was lying on his stomach, propped up on his elbows, looking out the door toward the other tent.

"Why did you move the tent after the girls spread it out?" Junior asked his dad.

"I wanted our tent to face theirs so we could keep an eye on it," Dr. Quicksolve said. "The ranger stopped by with a message for me. Apparently, a crazy fan has threatened Lucy," he explained.

The guys got up early the next morning to start a fire for breakfast. It was hot, and Junior took off the T-shirt he had slept in. He pulled the tent flap open and almost panicked for a second when he realized the girls were not in camp. Then he saw all of them standing down by the lake fishing. One of the twins was just reeling in a pretty big one.

They got the fire going, and Dr. Quicksolve asked Junior to help him get some water at the pump in the middle of the camp about a hundred yards away. "The fire will be okay," he said. Dr. Quicksolve carried four small canteens and Junior had the traditional, large, square, plastic camping jug.

As they walked to the water pump, they saw two men walking toward them from a dark truck parked back behind the trees. They were dressed exactly alike in dark shirts, jackets, and new dark blue jeans. They both were tall and thin. Each of them carried a kitchen pan. "I didn't see them before," Junior said.

"They came into camp about two this morning," Dr. Quicksolve said.

The two men got to the pump first and started filling their pans with water. One pumped the handle while the other held a pan under the spigot. The sudden burst of water surprised him, and he jumped away a little late. One loafer was soaked.

"Do you come here to camp a lot?" Dr. Quicksolve asked them.

"Yes," the one holding the pan said. "We do a lot of hiking." Junior must have not been hiding the fact that he was looking them over suspiciously. "Nothing wrong with a couple guys out camping, is there?" the man said directly to Junior.

"No. No," Junior said, "I camp with my friends a lot, too."

The man had small red spots across the back of his neck and across his forehead. "The mosquitoes are killers this year," he said. He scooped a little water from the pan and wiped it across the back of his neck.

When they got back to camp, Junior was surprised to see the girls were already putting the fish on the fire to cook.

This time it was Dr. Quicksolve who could not hide the look of concern on his face.

"Something wrong?" Lucy Looker asked him.

"Nothing that can't be handled," he said. "After breakfast I'm going to call Sergeant Shurshot to come out here. I want you to slip out of camp with the girls. I'll have her pretend she's you. We'll get some more help and wait for those guys to make their move."

"Make their move? What are you talking about?" Lucy said.

"You saw what I saw?" Junior said.

"Well," Dr. Quicksolve chuckled. "What did you see?"

What did you notice about the campers that might have made Dr. Quicksolve and Junior suspicious?

Answer on page 87.

Swimming Contest

Junior and his twin cousins, Flora and Fauna, were walking across the campground toward the sandy beach. They all were wearing their swimsuits, and they all had beach towels around their necks. The girls wore short terrycloth cover-ups.

"We were on the swimming team this past year," Flora said.

"That's great," Junior said. "You must be in good condition."

"That's for sure," Fauna said. "We had practice before and after school, even when it wasn't swimming season."

"Listen," Fauna said, winking at her sister. "I bet we

can swim farther than you can."

"Ha!" Junior said. "You know I'm a good swimmer. I'm older… and stronger, so how do you figure that?"

"Just do," Fauna said.

"Just do," Flora said.

"Okay," Junior said. "Listen. Let's put something on that bet. There are only two sodas left. Whoever wins gets the sodas, and the loser has to go get some more."

"Deal," Fauna said.

"Deal," Flora said.

"Okay. Let's have some rules," Junior said, looking out at the swimming area. "We'll go out to the corner of the roped-off area, into the deeper water, out of people's way. It's still shallow enough to stand up."

The girls looked out at the rope floating on the surface, marking the swimming area. It was about 200 yards from one corner to the other.

"You swim back and forth," Fauna said.

"Count your own laps out loud every time you get to the end," Flora said.

"Once you start you can't stop," Fauna said.

"If you touch the bottom you're done," Flora said.

"Okay. Let's go," Junior said.

They waded out to the corner of the swimming area and stood in a line facing the other side.

"One," Fauna said.

"Two," Flora said.

"Three," Fauna said.

"Go!" Junior said, stretching out and beginning his stroke. He swam casually, saving his energy. When he got to the end and touched the rope in the other corner, he said, "One!" Then he turned in the water without touching the bottom. He was puzzled to see

17

only Flora swimming toward him.

He looked around as well as he could between strokes and saw Fauna on the beach walking back toward camp. She already had her cover-up back on. He was confused about what was going on, figuring his cousins were up to one of their tricks again. He couldn't stop to protest very well without standing up and forfeiting the contest. He kept swimming, passing Flora somewhere in the middle each time he changed direction.

Junior kept looking up at the beach, and sure enough, he saw Fauna strolling back to the water's edge, carrying two bottles of soda. She was drinking from one of them. Junior swam about three more strokes. Then he stopped, stood up, and said, "Okay. You win. I'll get some more soda."

What had Junior decided?

Answer on page 88.

A Cash Withdrawal

Dr. J. L. Quicksolve saw Officer Longarm talking to a woman who was sitting in a green convertible parked in front of a Pitstop Convenience Store. Although it was a warm day, it was cloudy and misty. The convertible top was up. Dr. Quicksolve walked into the store and saw Sergeant Rebekah Shurshot talking with the clerk about the robbery.

The clerk said, "The guy got off his motorcycle right in front of the door. That woman in the green car was just walking out of the store. She held the door for him. Just as he got in, he flipped down the face mask on his helmet. He held his hand in his pocket like he had a gun. He told me to put the money into a bag. Then he made me lie down behind the counter. 'Don't get up until I'm gone!' he said.

"When I heard his motorcycle start, I stood up and ran to the door. He had backed his motorcycle up and was driving away. His face mask was flipped up, but I couldn't see his face. That woman in the car didn't see the robbery, I guess. I told her to wait for the police anyway. I think she was putting lipstick on or something. The glass door is tinted. You can't see in as well as you can see out."

Sergeant Shurshot's radio began to squawk. She got the message that a motorcycle rider had been stopped about three miles away. The description the clerk gave of the man's motorcycle and his black leather outfit matched, but he had no bag of money. "Of course, he could have tossed that anywhere," Sergeant Shurshot said.

The door swung open, and Officer Longarm walked in. Dr. Quicksolve saw the green car backing out of the parking space. "She gave me a description of…"

"Stop that car!" Dr. Quicksolve said. Officer Longarm turned and ran back outside, waving his arms at the woman.

"It will be interesting to hear her description," Dr. Quicksolve said.

What did Dr. Quicksolve suspect?

Answer on page 88.

Seven Hills Run

Dr. J. L. **Quicksolve sat** with his friend
Sergeant Rebekah Shurshot and Junior watching
the crowd of runners stampeding through the street in
front of them. The runners were men and women of
all ages, sizes, and shapes. They filled the street in a
huge colorful, rolling mass.

The Annual Community Bank Seven Hills Run
started downtown, early in the morning, at Community Bank's main building. Bright yellow cloth
"No Parking" signs covered the parking meters, and
ropes kept the spectators back on the sidewalks.
Barricades and volunteers kept the traffic off the
streets of the race route.

Like an ambling river, the route snaked its way
around the downtown area in its valley of tall build-

ings before it reached out to the first of several long, gradual inclines. Unlike the balanced ups and downs of a race that begins and ends at the same place, this one was quite torturous in that it only went up with a few level "breaks" here and there, which barely gave the runners a chance to catch their breath.

The famous detective enjoyed exercise, especially racing his bicycle, but he did not like running uphill. He preferred to celebrate this particular event by riding his bike to the donut shop on the edge of town where he could sit at the sidewalk tables in the shelter of a large canopy and watch the people racing by. Occasionally he would stand up, raise his coffee mug, and cheer on a friend he recognized in the race.

The donut shop was the only place open on this street this early except for a small branch of the Community Bank a couple stores downhill from the donut shop.

Dr. Quicksolve was eating a bagel instead of donuts

this year for his heart's sake. Sergeant Shurshot was sipping orange-flavored tea and nibbling a custard-filled éclair Junior had recommended. Junior was on his second donut.

The parade of colors filled the street like a collage of waving flags. Junior noticed bright colors were popular for the jogging suits, though there were several black-and-white outfits. One runner slowed to a walk and limped out of the middle of the flow of runners to the sidewalk. He bent down and rubbed his leg with both hands. He winced with pain.

"He should have warmed up better," Junior said.

"Yes, or maybe he was already sore when he started the race," Dr. Quicksolve said.

Only a few runners wore shorts and light shirts because of the cool and damp weather. It was still fairly dark because of the early hour and the clouds. It began to drizzle.

Suddenly a voice squawked, as it does, from Sergeant Shurshot's radio. A man dressed in a black-and-white running outfit had just robbed the bank two doors down.

"A copycat robber," Junior remarked, remembering a bank robbery attempt during a bicycle race he and his dad had been in at Kris Crossing.

His dad chuckled. "You might be right, son. That wouldn't make him the smartest criminal, though, would it?"

"What do you mean?" Junior asked.

"Well, if he's copying somebody who got caught…I guess he figures he's a little smarter," Dr. Quicksolve said.

"That's what they all think," Junior said.

Sergeant Shurshot stood up and pushed her chair up to the table. "Well, if he is smart, he will likely run downhill to a getaway car where he can slip away with the dispersing crowd." She turned and walked away, talking into her radio.

"That's one good theory," Dr. Quicksolve said. "Let's hop on our bikes and head the other way, at least to the corner. I think I might have spotted him."

Why didn't Dr. Quicksolve go along with Sergeant Shurshot? What did he think was going on?

Answer on pages 88–89.

Strike Up the Band

"**Mr. Sweeps is in a** lot of trouble," Prissy Powers told Junior Quicksolve, Dr. J. L. Quicksolve's son, as they walked down the hallway to their first-hour class.

"What happened?" Junior asked, concerned about his friend who had been a custodian at the school as long as Junior could remember.

"When I was coming in from soccer practice, I saw Sergeant Shurshot talking to John Bigdood and his brother in the parking lot. A couple of policemen took them away in handcuffs. They were caught with a van full of instruments from Mr. Tootlehorn's room," Prissy said.

"What does that have to do with Mr. Sweeps?" Junior asked.

"Sergeant Shurshot told me John said Mr. Sweeps sold him the instruments cheap. John said he and his brother were going to sell them for more. He claimed he wouldn't be stealing things in broad daylight," Prissy explained.

Junior laughed. "So he'd only steal things at night, eh? That sounds like something John would say. You know, he was smart enough to think of that argument ahead of time, in case he got caught. What did Mr. Sweeps say about all this?"

Prissy said, "I was with Sergeant Shurshot when she talked to him. She doesn't believe he could be involved either. He wouldn't risk his job like that."

"I don't think he'd have anything to do with John Bigdood," Junior said, "except when John has to help him clean the halls because he's gotten into trouble."

"Mr. Sweeps said John didn't help him clean last night. In fact, he said he didn't even clean the band room because he had to set up chairs for a meeting in

the gym. He said Mr. Tootlehorn always locks the door though," Prissy said.

"John plays drums in the band," Junior said. "Let's look at the band room before school starts."

They hurried to the band room. Prissy pulled the door open, and they saw Mr. Tootlehorn sitting at his desk with his face in his hands. "Oh!" he said. "I thought that door was locked. I came in the outside door from the parking lot. I was just sitting here wondering what's going to happen to Mr. Sweeps. The principal just called me from the office and told me what happened and that John Bigdood is blaming Mr. Sweeps. I can't believe..."

"I just pulled the door open," Prissy said. She walked back to the door to look at it. Junior walked to the back of the room where John Bigdood sat to play drums.

"Look what's here!" Prissy said.

"I can guess," Junior replied, bending down to pick up two small pieces of paper from under John's chair.

What had they found?

Answer on page 89.

A Will and a Way

Junior Quicksolve and his friend Derek came into the living room during an apparent lull in the conversation. A tall, dark-haired woman sat on the couch wiping her eyes. She had been crying. Dr. Quicksolve and his friend Fred Fraudstop looked at the boys. Fred noticed the boys were wearing Boy Scout uniforms. "Did you have a meeting today?" he asked Junior.

"Yes," Junior said. "We're working on a merit badge. We're studying the Pony Express and the U. S. Mail Service."

"Would you mind getting us something to drink?" Dr. Quicksolve asked his son.

Junior took the orders for sodas and tea. He and Derek went into the kitchen to get the drinks.

When they came back into the room, the woman was talking. "So it looks like this letter proves my father changed his will back in 1979 and is giving everything to my stepbrother. My husband and I were counting on Dad's promise to help him through medical school. Now he's going to have to drop out. I don't know how we're even going to pay off the loans we already have. There must be some way to deal with this. I know it's not what my dad wanted."

Junior Quicksolve looked down at the oak coffee table where the letter lay. He cocked his head to read the return address on the slightly tattered letter. He read, "Villains and Henchmen, Attorneys-at-Law, 26 Curbgutter Place, Valley Forge, PA 19432-2600."

"Look, Derek," he said.

Derek picked up the letter. "May I see that?" he said. He looked at the top of the letter and showed it to Junior.

"That is the will they said my dad wrote that changed who would inherit him," the woman said. Apparently she knew Junior often helped his father with cases, and she felt comfortable talking to these boys about her situation.

Junior and Derek looked at each other. Then Junior smiled and looked at the woman. "You're not going to have to worry about this will," he told her.

Fred Fraudstop jumped. "The ZIP code!" he said. "That's it! There was no ZIP code in 1979! Right? The will is a forgery!"

"No. There was a ZIP code," Junior said.

What did Junior and Derek know?

Answer on page 89.

Campus Cop

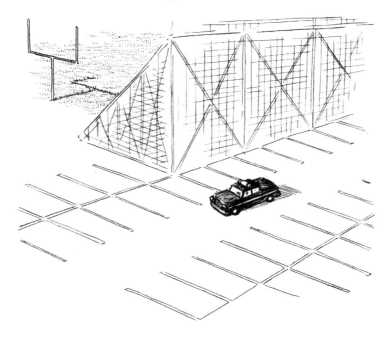

The campus police car turned into the long parking lot next to the huge university football stadium. The driver stopped the car to watch the customized purple pickup truck pull away from the far right end of the parking lot, near the stadium. He watched as the pickup drove out the exit.

The officer was a "campus cop" known by the local high school and college students as Officer Ron. He was a retired detective who got a job on the University Police Department. He was showing his friend Dr. J. L. Quicksolve around campus. "Being on campus is different…back in the patrol car," he said. "But a lot of the people getting in trouble on campus are from town, so I'm familiar with them. Like that guy in that pickup truck. We think he sells drugs over by the stadium."

They stopped, looked across the parking lot in both directions, and then turned left toward several cars parked at the opposite end of the parking lot. There were apparently two groups of teenage boys. They were standing near their cars, talking, drinking soft drinks, and playing catch with a football.

Officer Ron stopped the car before they reached either group. He pointed to the group on the left. He said, "Those guys are from Gardentown. The other group is from our high school here on the west side. They hang out here. No problem most of the time. But the guy in that purple truck parks down by the stadium and sells drugs. Let's go talk to these kids."

When they drove up to the Gardentown group, one of the boys walked up to the driver's side of the police car. Sweat was dripping from his face. His T-shirt was soaked, and he had a football in his hands.

"Did anybody drive over by the stadium when that purple truck was over there?" Officer Ron asked.

The boy said he wasn't sure, but he thought someone from the other group had been over there. He said he thought it was the maroon convertible with the top down.

Dr. Quicksolve noticed there were three cars in this group. Two were empty, and one, a black sports car, apparently had people inside it, but the windows were tinted and closed. The engine was running.

They quickly drove over to the hometown group, where one of the boys in the convertible said they had not gone over by the stadium, but he was sure the dark sports car from the other side had been over there.

They drove across the parking lot to the stadium end. In spite of the heat, Dr. Quicksolve rolled his window down and looked at the pavement. He looked up toward the other end where the boys were. "The sports car," he said.

What had Dr. Quicksolve seen?

Answer on page 89.

Mighty Neighborly

"**I only wanted to help out** my neighbors," Jack told Sergeant Rebekah Shurshot and Dr. J. L. Quicksolve. "Late last night I heard my neighbor's dog, Tyedye, barking. I knew the Farduckers weren't home, so I went out into the rainstorm to check things out for them. I walked around the house and looked around a bit. There was a light on, but I know they use a timer when they're gone. I didn't see that broken window. Everything looked all right to me."

Mary Littlethought, the neighbor from the other side of the house, said she woke up when the dog was barking, too. "I don't know how long he had been barking when I got up and looked out the window. I saw Jack walking away from the Farduckers' house. He was holding his hat down so it wouldn't blow away. The rain was just beginning to stop. I went back to my room and read most of the rest of the night because I couldn't sleep. Tyedye didn't bark anymore."

Timmy, the Farduckers' teenage nephew, who had called the police, was also there. He let them outside to the backyard. The dog barked furiously and tugged at the thick chain fastened to his doghouse at the end of the yard. "He barks at everybody, even the Farduckers," Timmy said.

They went into the house where Timmy showed them the broken window he said he discovered when he came to feed Tyedye that morning. The window was open. It looked like someone broke the glass to reach the latch and opened the window to climb inside. The carpeted floor was covered with broken glass. It looked dry except for muddy footprints that led into the bedroom and back.

"Aunt Fanny's jewelry has been taken," Timmy said. "I think he took Uncle Freddie's coin collection, too."

Noting that the tracks went directly to the bedroom and back to the window, Sergeant Shurshot said, "It looks bad for you, Timmy." She turned to Dr. Quicksolve and said, "The floor by the window would be wet from the rain if Jack had broken the window during the storm. It looks like Timmy was in the house when Jack came over to look around. After Jack left, he broke the window to make it look like Jack did it."

"Interesting idea," Dr. Quicksolve said, "but it doesn't work."

What's wrong with Sergeant Shurshot's theory?

Answer on pages 89–90.

Merger Murder

Dr. J. L. **Quicksolve** sat at the conference table with Lieutenant Rootumout, Sergeant Shurshot, District Attorney Henry Keesnot, and Mr. Keesnot's assistant, Shania Twitzel.

"We thought we had the murder of Tom Smitt solved until Cornet passed the lie-detector test. Now we're not so sure," Hank Keesnot said.

"Please start from the beginning," Dr. Quicksolve said.

"Well," Hank Keesnot began, "you know that Snoutshock.com and Nasalglitz have recently merged, forming the largest nose ring company in history."

"Virtually controlling the industry," Shania said.

"As always happens with mergers," Hank continued, "there is some consolidation and some people lose their jobs. They wanted to have just one company president, so either Tom Smitt or Carl Cornet was going to get the job, and the other one would lose out.

At the signing of the agreement, Tom Smitt used his favorite pen, as he always did for important papers. Almost immediately after signing, he fell dead."

"The doctor said he was poisoned. Someone put poison in the ink. He got it on his hand and died almost instantly," Shania said. "The doctor said the poison loses its potency in about an hour and is difficult to detect."

"Did Mr. Cornet use the same pen?" Dr. Quicksolve asked.

"Yes," Shania said. "He signed first, but apparently didn't touch the ink."

"We found out that Mr. Cornet's girlfriend just happened to be Claudia Mousepad, Tom Smitt's secretary! She's also the one who brought the pen to the table," Hank said. "It looked like Cornet and Claudia plotted to kill Smitt in order to get control of the company."

"But Cornet passed a lie-detector test, and Miss Mousepad refused to take one," Shania Twitzel said.

"It's hard to implicate Claudia if Cornet wasn't involved, especially since he used the pen first and might have been killed himself. We have a video of the signing if you want to see it. All the characters are there," Hank Keesnot said.

"If we can actually see them signing their names, we might be able to strengthen the case against Miss Mousepad," Dr. Quicksolve said.

What did Dr. Quicksolve plan to watch for on the videotape of the signing?

Answer on page 90.

Stolen Contract

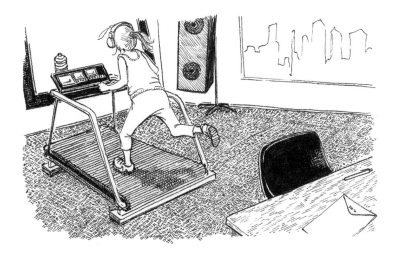

Dr. J. L. Quicksolve sat in a large, round, black leather chair shaped like a record. It was one of two matching chairs in the huge office of Gail Winds, president of Spinbig Records. Gail sat at her large oak desk in the middle of the room. Directly behind her was a large treadmill with all the electronic gizmos she needed for elaborate workouts. Behind that sat a large-screen television. To her right were a full-size refrigerator and a bar. To her left was a huge audio system. She did more than work in this room.

"I had just signed a huge contract with Ricky Roguehart. We were planning a giant party tonight to celebrate. I left the contract on my desk, and it just disappeared," Gail said.

"What do you think happened to it?" Dr. Quicksolve asked.

"I think someone stole it!" she said curtly.

"I mean when and how?" Dr. Quicksolve said patiently.

"It must have been taken while I was exercising," Gail said. "I always use the treadmill and watch the news at noon. Someone must have come in and taken it. Now Ricky denies we had a contract. He's going with another company. I think they made him a bigger offer and paid someone to steal the contract."

Dr. Quicksolve walked over to the treadmill and turned it on. It hummed noisily.

"It gets a lot of use. It helps me relax," Gail said.

"Who knew you had the contract?" Dr. Quicksolve asked.

"My vice-president. I called him. He's out of town. Other than that, there were only two people. Charlotte, my secretary, got it from Edie. Edie works downstairs. She got it from the delivery service. She just started work today. I don't really know her. Of course, everyone knew it was coming. This is a big disappointment for us."

"Your secretary's desk is right outside the office, right?" Dr. Quicksolve said.

"Yes, but she takes her lunch any time around twelve. She said she didn't see anyone come in. Do you think someone hired Edie to steal it?" Gail said, pointing back toward the office door.

"No," Dr. Quicksolve said. "Edie is not the one I suspect."

What did Dr. Quicksolve think happened?

Answer on page 90.

Winter Break

Dr. J. L. Quicksolve sat on the passenger
side of Sergeant Rebekah Shurshot's patrol car.
He sipped his tea from a paper cup. He held a donut
in his other hand. They were parked out a little from
the curb to avoid the snowdrift in front of the East
Main Street Donut Shop. A city salt truck sped by,
heading west. It sprayed the police car with salt pellets.
They sat there with the engine rumbling quietly,
watching the cold wind blow the snow around.

"That's the first salt truck we've seen this morning,"
Sergeant Shurshot said.

"They're getting the main roads first," Dr.
Quicksolve said.

Their morning break was interrupted with the news

of a break-in at a hardware store about four miles away on West Main Street. Sergeant Shurshot turned the flashing lights on the roof of her black-and-white patrol car, made a U-turn, and headed toward the scene of the robbery.

Half a block from their destination, they passed a narrow, icy side street where they saw two uniformed officers escorting a man in a dark coat and hat up the middle of the street toward them. Sergeant Shurshot parked at the corner, and they got out of the car. One of the policemen was Officer Longarm. "Here's our best suspect," he said.

"I was coming this way, up the hill," the man said. "I don't know what you're talking about. I wasn't running away."

Dr. Quicksolve looked past the man, down the steep hill at the snow-covered sidewalks. He could see down the isolated street. There were no cross streets where someone might have been waiting to pick up the robber.

"The man you want ran down this street all right," the suspect continued. "He looked scared. He turned left down there a block or two and ran into somebody's yard," the suspect said before Officer Longarm's partner led him away.

"What was taken?" Dr. Quicksolve asked Officer Longarm.

"Cash," he said. "The owner of the store was unlocking the door. Somebody knocked him down and grabbed the wallet out of his pocket. He said he had about $200 to put in the cash register. When he got up, he just saw a glimpse of somebody rounding this corner. It all took place in just a few minutes. He called 911 on his cell phone, and we all got here almost immediately."

"He has money on him," Longarm's partner said when he came back from quickly questioning the suspect and turning him over to two other officers who had arrived on the scene. "It was in his wallet. I don't know if we can prove it isn't his money."

"Get your movie camera out of the car, and let's go for a walk," Dr. Quicksolve said to Sergeant Shurshot.

What did Dr. Quicksolve want the camera for?

Answer on pages 90–91.

Sayahh.com

Dr. J. L. **Quicksolve parked** his yellow VW Beetle in front of the small gray building. The large sign above the door read "Sayahh.com." The detective went in to talk to the owner of the business, Phil Flemm, about the robbery.

"This is an e-business. We sell autographed tongue depressors over the Internet," Mr. Flemm explained.

"How's business? Is there a big demand for auto-graphed tongue depressors?" Dr. Quicksolve asked.

"Not right now," Mr. Flemm said. "We aren't making a profit. But, of course, that's expected when you're in an Internet business. Right now we're going for market share. Our stock is going through the ceiling. It will all come together soon. We've had a few buyout offers, but we're holding out."

"Tell me about the robbery," Dr. Quicksolve said.

"We have a suspect, but let's go back to my office," Mr. Flemm said. "By the way, this is Paul Deels." He indicated the only other person in the room. Paul sat at his desk, typing at a computer. He stopped and shook Dr. Quicksolve's hand when he was introduced.

Dr. Quicksolve and Phil Flemm went back to his office. "I only have two employees. Paul works up there during the day, and Julie Johnson works at the other desk in the evening. She's my suspect."

"Go ahead and tell me what you think happened," Dr. Quicksolve said.

"It's simple," Phil said. "Ten thousand dollars' worth of autographed tongue depressors were out in the front office when Paul and I left yesterday afternoon. When we came in this morning, they were gone."

"Who has keys?" Dr. Quicksolve asked.

"I don't let anyone use my keys. I only have one key, and I keep it," Phil said.

"How does Julie lock up at night without a key?" Dr. Quicksolve asked.

"She just locks the door from the inside and closes it. She doesn't need a key to do that. Of course, she could've made a mistake and left the door open. I called her, though, and she said she's sure she closed it. There's no sign of a break-in, so it's pretty obvious she took the depressors. I like Julie, and this is very upsetting."

"Let's look around the front office and think about this," Dr. Quicksolve said.

They walked out to the front office. It was very stark. There were only two desks with computers on them.

"Your stock of tongue depressors?" Dr. Quicksolve asked.

"They all were taken. We're waiting for more. Most of them, actually, are shipped directly to our customers. We never see them," Phil said.

"May I look around?" Dr. Quicksolve asked.

"Go ahead. Check out anything you want," Phil said.

Dr. Quicksolve opened the drawers of Julie's desk and searched them carefully. One drawer was full of *Dr. Quicksolve Mini-Mysteries,* by Jim Sukach.

"She has good taste," Dr. Quicksolve said. Then he stepped over to Paul's desk. "Do you mind?" he asked, indicating that he would like to look in Paul's desk. Paul seemed a little nervous, but he said it would be okay.

"Julie didn't leave herself an alibi," Dr. Quicksolve said as he searched through Paul's desk. "It seems too easy to believe she did it."

In Paul's desk, Dr. Quicksolve didn't find anything unusual except a box of straws, twenty-six auto-graphed tongue depressors, and a few tools—a hammer, a pair of pliers, a screwdriver, and a small can of oil.

"I paid for those," Paul said. "I collect some of the rare ones. I have receipts."

"Do you oil them?" Dr. Quicksolve said.

What did Dr. Quicksolve suspect?

Answer on page 91.

Cookie Jar Caper

Dr. J. L. Quicksolve could see nothing but the wall when he stood beside the aluminum ladder that extended up to the bedroom window of Wilbur and Ruthie Resident's home. He did notice part of the wall had been painted recently. The large bushes next to the neighbor's house prevented him from stepping back and taking a better look at what appeared to be the window entrance the burglar had used. He reached his foot carefully up to the second rung of the ladder to avoid the encroaching shrubbery and climbed up. The bedroom window was wide open, and he climbed into the house just as the burglar would have done.

Downstairs, Ruthie Resident was telling Sergeant Rebekah Shurshot that she drove her children, Randy

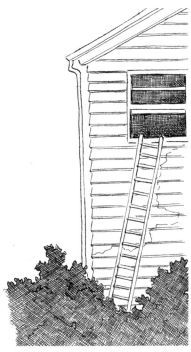

and Rufus, to school every morning. She left today, as usual, at 7:45 and returned home at 8:05 to see her ladder out of her garage and propped next to the house. She went upstairs to find the window wide open. She had left it only slightly open for the sake of fresh air. She always kept the downstairs windows locked.

Nothing seemed to be disturbed until she checked her cookie jar money, about $200, and found it gone. That's when she called the police.

"Mrs. Resident called police headquarters about the same time as her neighbor on the side of the house where the ladder is standing," Sergeant Shurshot told Dr. Quicksolve. "Miss Sally Stretchitout said she was just getting back from jogging when she saw the ladder and became suspicious. She said she jogged about five miles every morning. She also gave us the license number of a car that was driving away just as she turned the corner onto this street."

"I would like to see her," Dr. Quicksolve said.

"I want to look at that ladder again," Sergeant Shurshot said. "I will see if Miss Stretchitout can come over here."

Sergeant Shurshot walked out just as an older

woman in a cotton dress came into the house. "I saw the police car," she said.

"This is Mrs. Pringle," Ruthie said. "She lives on the other side of our house. Mrs. Pringle, Miss Stretchitout, and I usually have coffee at this time every morning." Ruthie turned to Mrs. Pringle. "There's been a burglary. My cookie jar money."

"Oh, my!" said Mrs. Pringle. "Sally warned you about keeping your money there just last week!"

"Have you been painting your house?" Dr. Quicksolve asked Ruthie.

"My husband has been painting a little bit at a time. He's out of town right now."

Sergeant Shurshot walked into the house with an attractive, athletic young woman who wore an old pair of jeans, a baseball cap with a ponytail sticking out the back, and an old, plaid work shirt that she had tied up with a knot in front, exposing a flat, muscular stomach. "This is Miss Stretchitout," Sergeant Shurshot told Dr. Quicksolve. "Also, I got a call on my radio. They found the suspect. He's from Mexico. He's visiting relatives on the next block. He just got into this country for the first time early this morning. He rented a car at the airport. The license number matches the one

Miss Stretchitout turned in earlier. He had nearly $300 in cash on him. It sounds like he's the man."

Dr. Quicksolve seemed to ignore Sergeant Shurshot's last statement and said, "Was that ladder outside when you left, Ruthie?"

"No. I am sure it wasn't. It was in the garage. It hangs up right in front of my car."

"Was the garage door open?" he asked.

"Yes. I leave it open. The door to the house is locked, and I'm gone such a short time. I don't usually worry about it," Ruthie said.

"Well, We've got the man, and we've got the money back," Sergeant Shurshot said.

"I don't think so," Dr. Quicksolve said. "There are several reasons to suspect someone else over our international friend."

Who? What reasons?

Answer on pages 91–92.

Kidnapped Kicker

An ice cream shop was a strange place to solve a crime, but it was where Dr. J. L. Quicksolve and Junior usually ended up after Junior's soccer games. This time it was well after the game because of the kidnapping of Worthington Lesley Cashbin during the second half of the game. Junior was eating a foot-long Coney dog besides his usual ice cream treat. Lieutenant Rootumout had met them at the ice cream shop to talk about the kidnapping.

"It's very strange," Lieutenant Rootumout said. "Worthington's parents found the kidnapper's note in his soccer bag after he disappeared. Tell me what you saw, Junior. By the way, isn't Worthington older than you are? How can you be on the same soccer team?"

"Yes. Worthless is...," Junior began.

"Worthless?" Lieutenant Rootumout asked.

"Oh, that's what we call him. He's a good sport about his being rich and everything. Lately, though, he's been complaining about his parents reducing his allowance because of low grades. But, to answer your question, he's sixteen. I 'play up.' They let a few younger guys play with an older group if they're good enough.

"Anyway, it's a short story. We were ahead three to one. We scored three goals in the first half. We were lucky because the other team had to shoot into the sun and against the wind. Now it was our turn to have those problems. Worthless took a shot at the goal. He's usually a good shot, but this time it went high over the top of the goal. He ran after the ball into the trees and brush behind the goal. He never came out. His bodyguards ran back there pretty quickly, but he was gone."

"Those bodyguards said they had been watching for strangers or suspicious characters. They claim they always do. They hadn't seen anyone suspicious at all," Lieutenant Rootumout said.

"What did the note ask for?" Dr. Quicksolve asked the lieutenant.

"It asked for $10,000," Lieutenant Rootumout said.

"That's not much money for the return of a multi-millionaire's son," Dr. Quicksolve noted.

"No, it isn't," Lieutenant Rootumout agreed.

"It looks fishy, doesn't it?" Dr. Quicksolve said.

"It sure does," Junior piped in.

"Do you realize what was so unusual that happened during the game?" Dr. Quicksolve asked his son.

What did Dr. Quicksolve suspect? What was unusual about the soccer game?

Answer on page 92.

Another Warehouse Murder

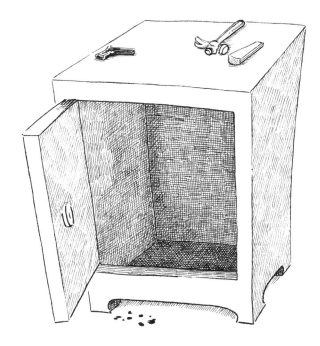

D r. J. L. Quicksolve looked down at the outline of a man drawn on the gray warehouse floor. A puddle of blood was all that was left of the victim, Dan Gomer, the owner of the business. Twenty feet away sat the empty black safe. The safe door was wide open, apparently forced open with the hammer and chisel that lay on top of it next to a small semi-automatic pistol. Small drops of blood dotted the concrete floor in front of the safe.

"He was shot in the back," Officer Beekerjar, the police department science expert, told Dr. Quicksolve and Sergeant Rebekah Shurshot. "The bullet went right through his heart. It's lodged there in the door." He pointed back to the safe. "Even though the tools and gun are here, there's not much evidence. They've been wiped clean. There aren't any fingerprints. The numbers have been filed off the gun. Since it was left, it was probably stolen anyway."

Sergeant Shurshot looked at the outline on the floor that marked how the body was found. She walked over to the safe and looked at the damage that was done to open it. "Why didn't the robber just make Gomer open the safe? Why shoot somebody for... what was it...$70?"

"Maybe he tried," Dr. Quicksolve said, "and Gomer tried to get away. Or maybe Gomer walked in on the guy while he was trying to open it. Then he turned to run away. It's hard to tell. We do have..."

Lieutenant Rootumout burst through the door. "We've got two suspects!" he said. "As usual," he added proudly. "Our officers have been doing pretty well lately. When the neighborhood officer reported the crime on duty, two separate officers on patrol each caught a suspect speeding away from here in opposite directions. Each of the suspects is handcuffed and sitting in a squad car

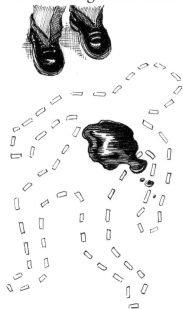

out in front of the warehouse right now. Do you want to talk to them?"

"I guess one of the officers can tell us which one did it," Dr. Quicksolve said.

"How can…?" Lieutenant Rootumout began.

"As a matter of fact, either one of the officers' reports will probably tell us if it was his guy or the other suspect. Of course, the final decision is up to Officer Beekerjar," Dr. Quicksolve said.

Huh?

Answer on pages 92–93.

Following Cecil Sapp

Frank Conwise was the tall, dark-haired gentleman in a tan suit who approached famous detective Dr. J. L. Quicksolve as he walked off the airplane at the busy Fort Lauderdale Airport. He was a friend of Dr. Quicksolve's who was working as chief of security for Oceanside Banks.

"Samuel Sapp, president of Oceanside Banks, asked me to invite you down here to enjoy a little stay in our sunny town and help us with the problem we discussed over the phone," Frank said.

"You want me to spend some time with the bank president's son," Dr. Quicksolve said.

"That is right...Cecil Sapp. He's had some problems. His father, Samuel Sapp, is a wealthy and

generous man. He gives a lot of money to the poor and organizations like the Salvation Army and the Boy Scouts.

"But people think Cecil is young and naive, someone easy to fool. Cecil is a nice guy. Sometimes people take advantage of nice guys. He's just beginning to learn the banking business out in the real world now that he's finished with college. He likes to think everyone is a good person, and he has trouble spotting a real con man. Cecil has already lost money for himself and the company. He's become something of an embarrassment to his father, and every con man in Florida seems to know he's an easy mark."

The next morning, Cecil Sapp, a tall, thin, amiable young man with blond hair and a smiling face, stood at the bank window where he was ready to work as a cashier in one of the Oceanside Banks. Dr. Quicksolve sat beside him. Things went well in the beginning.

Dr. Quicksolve sat watching Cecil dealing with the customers who drove up to their positions outside the window and placed their deposits and other business into cylinders that they put in receptacles that went racing through long tubes that were brought almost magically to Cecil's desk.

Dr. Quicksolve looked back over his shoulder toward the front door of the bank where he saw a man enter wearing sunglasses, a long coat, and a baseball cap. The man stopped to look around. Then he walked out smiling after he saw Cecil working at the drive-thru window.

"There's one to watch," Dr. Quicksolve said, pointing the man out to Cecil. They both turned to watch through the large front windows of the bank. They saw the man leave and climb into a red sports car.

A few minutes later, that same man in that same red car was outside their window placing something into one of the cylinders. It came whistling along the long tube and appeared in front of them with a muffled whoosh. Cecil opened the cylinder and looked at the Oceanside Bank deposit slip and a check from another bank written out for $400, less $200 cash back. The check number was 118, and it had that day's date. The check was written to Thomas Trout. That name was also on the deposit slip. Cecil started to count out $200.

"Ask him to come into the bank," Dr. Quicksolve said.

"But he's one of our customers," Cecil objected. "He has a deposit slip and…" Cecil punched a few computer keys. "He has enough money in his account to cover the whole check."

"There are several reasons," the detective said, "besides his suspicious behavior."

What did Dr. Quicksolve mean?

Answer on page 93.

Callahan and Callahan

A s they walked down the hall at Police Headquarters, Sergeant Rebekah Shurshot explained the situation to Dr. J. L. Quicksolve. "We don't know if Casey Callahan is telling us the truth about being kidnapped by Carl Callahan, or if he's setting Carl up to get him out of the way so he can take over Callahan and Callahan."

"Are they brothers?" Dr. Quicksolve asked.

"No. They're not even related. They met at a convention a few years ago and thought it would be funny if they started a business together and called it Callahan and Callahan. They did start a business, but they argued about whose name was first on the sign and about nearly everything else ever since the business opened. There was a lot of animosity. They each wanted to get the business away from the other guy."

Sergeant Shurshot pushed open an unmarked door, and they walked into a small observation room. On the other side of what Dr. Quicksolve knew was a one-way mirror sat Casey Callahan. Lieutenant Rootumout was questioning him. Casey seemed quite composed for someone who had just escaped from a kidnapper who might well have intended to murder him. He sat calmly in his red woolen cardigan, smoking a pipe, and he began telling his story.

"I was working very late at the office. If we're going to have a successful business with a fancy office, somebody's got to do the work to pay for all that expensive carpeting and furniture and that fancy equipment my partner orders. He thinks I'm in charge of bringing the money in and it's his job to spend it.

"Anyway, I was alone in the building when Callahan…we call each other Callahan…when Callahan, walks in. He says, 'It's over, Callahan,' and he pulls something out of his pocket and hits me over the head. It was some kind of a sap, a sock full of pellets or something. Anyway, it knocked me out of the chair. I was pretty dizzy. He tied my hands behind my back. He tied my feet together and dragged me by my feet out to his car.

"He took me to a little motel out in the country and put me in a room out toward the back, away from the street, where nobody would see us. I kept asking him what he was doing and why he was doing it. I said, 'You won't get away with this, Callahan!'

"He didn't tell me anything! All he'd say was, 'It's

over, Callahan!' Anyway, he tied me to the bed and left. When he was gone, I managed to get the ropes loose and get out of there. I got away from there because I was afraid he'd come back. When I got home, I called the police. That's all there is. I'm sure he'll deny everything. Maybe the judge will let me have my business, though."

"Lieutenant Rootumout has a listening device in his ear," Sergeant Shurshot told Dr. Quicksolve. "We can talk to him. Do you want him to ask Callahan anything?"

"Yes," said Dr. Quicksolve. "Have him ask if the

custodian had finished before this all happened. Then have Lieutenant Rootumout ask him what motel and what room he was taken to. That will go a long way in helping us find out if he's telling the truth or if he's trying to frame his partner."

How can they tell if the story is true with that information?

Answer on page 93.

Mystery Train

"So many artists try** to capture the beauty of fall, but nothing can match this," Sergeant Rebekah Shurshot said, looking out the window of the train as it raced through the beautiful forests of the Michigan Upper Peninsula.

"It almost overwhelms the senses," Fred Fraudstop said.

"There's a deer!" Junior Quicksolve shouted.

Six friends were together on this Fall Tour Train to see the exciting colors of a Michigan autumn, but they were there for another reason, too. It had been Sergeant Shurshot's idea—a game. "We'll have our

own 'Mystery Train,'" she said. "We'll see who has the best idea for solving the mystery!"

"That won't be fair," Junior had said. "Dad will guess all the answers."

"No, he won't," Sergeant Shurshot said. "We will make him the judge."

So there they were, chugging across the beautiful countryside. They watched the colorful sunset as darkness began to blanket the collage of colors flying by. Dinner had been served, and everyone was enjoying warm apple or cherry pie desserts or just sipping coffee or cider.

Sergeant Shurshot stood up and said, "It's time for the first question." The four contestants listened carefully. They were all friends—Junior, Fred Fraudstop, Officer Beekerjar, and Benjamin Clayborn Blowhard.

Sergeant Shurshot told the story.

Two elderly sisters and a parakeet who lived together in a crowded little apartment in New York City inherited an Internet company, Birdbottom.com. The company, which recycled old newspapers and distributed them to pet shops around the country for use on the bottom of birdcages, was very successful and very valuable. Although there seemed to be plenty of money to go around, the sisters were understandably disturbed about having to share the money and the decision-making with a parakeet.

One night the sound of a shot rang out from the apartment. Neighbors called the police, who arrived immediately to find the two old ladies each sitting in her own rocking chair, rocking madly. They were staring at the birdcage, where the parakeet lay dead on the floor of the wire birdcage suspended from the ceiling. He had been shot. Between the two ladies was a large goldfish bowl on a small table. The goldfish swam in circles, unconcerned by the silver revolver that lay at the bottom of the bowl.

When the police asked what happened, each lady calmly pointed to her sister and said, "She did it."

"The question," Sergeant Shurshot said, "is, 'How can anyone prove who shot the bird?'"

"Well," Benjamin Clayborn Blowhard said, "the angle of the shot will tell you who fired the gun."

"Who owned the gun?" Junior asked. "That might be a clue."

"Motive," said Fred Fraudstop. "That might tell you which one was most desperate…like who needed the money the most."

Officer Beekerjar said, "Who shot the gun is what matters. We could figure that out right away."

"Well," Sergeant Shurshot said, turning to Dr. Quicksolve. "Who do you think is right?"

What did Dr. Quicksolve say?

Answer on pages 93–94.

Mystery Train Two

"**H**ooray for Officer Beekerjar. He solved the first mystery," Sergeant Shurshot said. "Now he's ineligible for the second question. He did have an advantage, but so does everyone else here—the son of the famous Dr. J. L. Quicksolve; an experienced insurance investigator; a well-traveled adventurer. There are three of you left—Junior Quicksolve, Fred Fraudstop, and Benjamin Clayborn Blowhard."

As the train whistled their passing through another little Michigan town, Sergeant Shurshot set the scene for the next mystery story.

Mrs. Monty Blanchard Beauregard of the Memphis Beauregards was plagued with a haunting obsession for Swiss chocolates. Even though she was concerned about keeping her girlish figure, she would have one small, delicious chocolate bar flown in by jet every morning. Before she would even eat her breakfast, she would stand out on the front porch of her mansion, waiting for the small delivery truck, more welcome to her than the sunrise. Then she would take the delivery herself and rush her little treasure up to her room where she would place it in a large, ornately carved wooden box.

Though she would often think about her precious little chocolate bar and speak of it lovingly, she had disciplined herself severely and refused to eat it until evening fell, her day was finished, and she could change into her pajamas and ceremoniously unlock her wooden box and munch away at her delicious chocolate.

Mrs. Beauregard loved to have visitors—so many visitors that they could hardly be kept track of everywhere. That proved to be a huge part of the problem when the treasured chocolate bar disappeared.

The bloodcurdling scream that shot through the walls filled the valley and continued, as if to saturate all time and space, and it seared the ears and pierced the heart with such savage human loss that the servants, who were knocked to the floor by the impact, knew immediately what must have happened. They composed themselves quickly and boldly hurried to Mrs. Beauregard's room.

"Shall we call the police?" her maid said.

"No time! No time!" Mrs. Beauregard screamed. "Search! Search!" she shouted.

"The room was locked?" the butler asked.

"Of course! Of course!" Mrs. Beauregard screamed. "The secret door!" the butler said.

The chauffeur immediately walked to a large bookcase and pulled one side of it away from the wall. It was a hinged door to a hidden passageway. The light of the room flooded into the dark entry and spotlighted a small candy wrapper lying on the floor like the murdered heroine in a Shakespearean tragedy.

"Eeeeiii!" screamed Mrs. Beauregard.

"Find the thief!" she growled with the voice of a demon.

The servants poured into the park passageway, separating this way and that.

In a surprisingly short time they all returned. Each servant had collared a guest who had been hiding in a different offshoot of the secret tunnels that spidered through the huge house. The maid held Miss Scarletti's arm behind her back. She was caught clutching a candlestick tightly in both hands. The butler found Colonel Catsup carrying a long crowbar. The chauffeur caught Mr. Green with a small hatchet. The mansion cook returned with a young boy carrying a large screwdriver.

Miss Scarletti said she pulled a book out of the bookcase in her room and the wall opened up. She was

using the candle to find her way as she explored the tunnels out of feminine curiosity.

Colonel Catsup said he heard a noise in the wall, found the opening to the passageway, and went searching for a possible burglar with a crowbar he found in the tunnel.

Mr. Green said he thought he was going into the shower to turn the water on before he undressed, but after he took his glasses off. He said he always kept a hatchet with him when he used a shower in a strange place ever since he saw the movie *Psycho*. Without his glasses, he somehow ended up in the passageway instead of the shower.

The young boy said he was the paperboy coming to collect. He said he knocked on the door and thought he heard someone say come in. He came in and heard another noise, and a panel opened up in the wall. He stepped in, and the panel closed behind him. He had the screwdriver because he had been having trouble with his bicycle chain.

"Well!" Sergeant Shurshot said when she finished telling the story. "How can we tell 'whodunit?'"

"I usually find that the most dangerous one is the one who appears to be the weakest, and the most guilty one is the one who appears to be the most innocent. Therefore, I think it was the little boy," Benjamin Clayborn Blowhard announced.

Fred Fraudstop said, "I don't see how the paperboy would know about the candy bar, so I don't think he did it. The hatchet story is pretty strange, but if he really wore glasses and didn't have them on, his story sounds almost believable. That movie did scare a lot of people. On the other hand, the guy with the crowbar looks very suspicious to me. You don't just happen to find crowbars lying around. I think he brought it in intending to steal the candy bar."

Finally Junior said, "I think we are supposed to concentrate on the question. How can we tell who did it? I don't know the answer, but I think it might have more to do with what they each had in their hands, rather than who they are. That is the most peculiar part of the story to me."

"Well, Dr. Quicksolve, who has the best answer?"

"I think I know who has the best answer, but if I say what I think, I am going to look partial this time. So I think we should let Officer Beekerjar decide who is the winner."

"Apparently, we agree about that," Officer Beekerjar said.

How can we tell who did it?

Answer on page 94.

Defining Moment

Ring! **Ring!** Dr. J. L. Quicksolve reached up with his left hand to the cell phone that lay next to his pillow in the dark sleeping compartment of the train. "Okay," he said into the phone. Then he pulled back the curtain, threw his legs around so he was sitting up on the edge of the bunk, and stretched a minute before he headed for the bathroom.

The cell phones were Benjamin Clayborn Blowhard's idea. He said that because of the limited facilities, they should have a plan and use the cell phones to let each other know when the facilities were available in the morning. That way everyone wouldn't end up standing around in his nightclothes waiting for one another. They all thought that idea made sense. Of course, Blowhard set it up so he would be the last one called

and could sleep in the longest.

They all sat together at two tables for breakfast in the dining car. There had been little talking through the meal, and Blowhard kept things on a serious note by asking Dr. Quicksolve, "So why did you leave the police force? I have never heard the story."

Usually reluctant to talk about it, Dr. Quicksolve surprised his friends by going right ahead with the story. "I wasn't exactly asked to leave the force," he said, "but I decided it was the best thing to do. I had a partner at the time, a good friend though a little eccentric, Elliott Savant. Some people actually thought we were brothers. The Policy Board and others seemed to think I put his life in jeopardy. I didn't think so. Elliott didn't think so."

He went on to tell the story of how they were called to a robbery in progress. Elliott got out of the police car first, just as a man with a gun came out of a small bank. The bandit raised his gun toward Dr. Quicksolve's partner. Dr. Quicksolve drew his gun and shot the man's gun hand before he had it leveled at his target.

Elliott boasted that Dr. Quicksolve had saved his life. The Policy Board saw things differently. The policy for using a gun in a life-threatening situation was to aim for the center of the torso, the largest target and the best way to be as sure as possible that you hit the person you are aiming at. In the intense pressure of a life-or-death incident, it is considered the right thing to do.

Dr. Quicksolve disagreed. "He saved my life!" Elliott had insisted at the hearing. "He wasn't taking any chances. I've seen Dr. Quicksolve shoot quarters out of the air—as many as ten in a row—shooting from two revolvers, without missing! He shoots skeet with a handgun! If he aimed for the gun hand, he would hit the gun hand as surely as he could have shot the zipper off the man's jacket! The policy does not apply to him."

Some disagreed. "Policy is policy," they said.

As we intently watch a group of people making an emotional decision together, we can tell who agrees by the small clues, such as a slight nod or a furrowed forehead. It looked like Dr. Quicksolve had the three votes he needed to stay on the force. But it was one of the nodders who asked the defining question. "Dr. Quicksolve, if you are allowed to stay on the force, will you promise to follow department policy in these situations?"

Dr. Quicksolve answered firmly without hesitating. "No, I cannot."

"Even if the life of your partner is at stake?" another board member asked angrily. "You're not the Lone Ranger! You're not making a movie!"

This time Dr. Quicksolve was slow to respond. "I want to thank you all for helping me to see things more clearly," he said. "I do not argue with department policy. I simply cannot do it. No, I'm not the Lone Ranger." He smiled. "But, like the Lone Ranger, I think it's time for me to ride off into the sunset."

Sergeant Shurshot had finished the story. Everyone was quiet. They decided to move to the passenger car and enjoy the scenery. They had all just settled into their seats when the train stopped. "It must be Rogers City," Sergeant Shurshot said.

Suddenly the doors at both ends of the train car opened, and two gunmen wearing dark ski masks entered. "Hands up! Hands up!" they yelled.

"What is this?" Blowhard shouted.

"A robbery?" Sergeant Shurshot said.

"Shut up!" one of the robbers said.

"What are you two planning to do with those guns?" Dr. Quicksolve asked.

"Just give him your money," one of the robbers said. The other one walked along with a sack, making sure he got everyone's wallet and jewelry.

"That's not much of a haul," Dr. Quicksolve said calmly as he dropped his wallet into the sack.

"How did you decide to rob this train here at the Rogers City train station?" Fred Fraudstop asked.

"What are you guys, mystery writers or something?" the first robber said.

"Something like that," Dr. Quicksolve said.

"Leave that chapter out," the second robber said. No one laughed at that old joke.

"Let's get out of here before the train starts!" the first robber said.

"Wait," Dr. Quicksolve said. He pulled a couple dollars from his shirt pocket. "Here's a little more." The robber held up the sack for Dr. Quicksolve like a masked trick-or-treater. Then both desperadoes backed to the doors before they turned to run.

"Well. A real mystery," Sergeant Shurshot said when the bandits were gone.

No one asked the obvious question.

What was the obvious question?

Answer on pages 94–95.

Elliott Savant

"**Who is this Detective** Elliott Savant?" Benjamin Clayborn Blowhard asked no one in particular.

No one in particular answered. The four of them sat in a row on a long bench, resting in the shade of a large tree watching the polar bears play in the water of their area at the zoo.

Finally Junior spoke up. "He's unusual."

"He's different," Sergeant Shurshot said.

"He looks kind of 'lost in space,'" Ben said. "Is he a good detective?"

"He's very good at detecting," Dr. Quicksolve said.

"Does that mean he's a good detective?" Ben insisted, sensing his question had not really been answered.

Silence again.

"He knows things," Sergeant Shurshot said slowly.

"Oh?" Ben said.

"He knows things he shouldn't know," Sergeant Shurshot said.

"He sees things other people don't see," Junior said.

Sergeant Shurshot smiled. "And he doesn't see things everybody else sees."

"He's a good detective," Dr. Quicksolve finally said.

"Like you?" Ben asked bluntly.

Junior laughed. "No. Not like Dad!"

"He always has some amazing insight," Sergeant Shurshot said enthusiastically. Then she said, "But he doesn't always solve the case."

"Sometimes he does," Junior said. "Like the Meditators."

"That's a good example," Sergeant Shurshot said. "The Meditators' Incident."

The Meditators' Incident

There seemed to be a lot of confusion in the large, quiet living room of the secluded house that stood on a high hill that overlooked the city. It belonged to Pigeon Quirk, who sat, legs crossed with his arms stretched in front of him, palms resting on his knees. He was apparently unconscious. Four lace doilies lay out in front of him, forming a large circle on the carpeted floor of the otherwise empty room.

Dr. J. L. Quicksolve looked around at the room. Sergeant Rebekah Shurshot, Officer Boysenberry, and two emergency medics seemed to be waiting to hear what Dr. Quicksolve had to say. The other person in the room, Detective Elliott Savant, who looked like a tall, skinny Albert Einstein in trench coat and galoshes, bent down and looked Mr. Quirk square in the face. Mr. Quirk, eyes wide open in some kind of trance, did not blink. Elliott did—twice. Then he stood up, left the room, and walked into the kitchen.

"Well?" Dr. Quicksolve said to the two medics. They might have been twins. They both looked very much like mice. The small man spoke first. "They apparently were meditating. We took out the four dead ones. They were sitting on the doilies. I suppose Mr. Quirk is sitting on a doily too. I don't think that's what killed them, though."

"Death by doily?" the woman medic interjected in a squeaky voice, "I don't think so!" She stared at her partner. Then she turned to Dr. Quicksolve and said, "Starvation! They died of starvation. We'd better wake him up before he goes too!"

"No! No!" The little man said. "His spirit might not be in there!" He bent down and looked into Mr. Quirk's eyes as Detective Savant had done. "Knock, knock!" he yelled. "Anybody home?" He looked up. "I don't think anybody's home," he said.

"You're not home!" his partner said.

82

Sergeant Shurshot spoke quietly. "I think you had better get Mr. Quirk to a hospital."

"Can't move him!" said Mr. Medic. "His spirit might come back, and he won't be home!"

"Your brain needs a home!" Miss Medic said.

Suddenly the room was filled with the aroma of toasted bread—cinnamon and raisin bread.

"This guy may be dying and Detective Savant is having a snack," Sergeant Shurshot whispered to Dr. Quicksolve.

The strong smell of peanut butter wafted through the room, mingling with the smell of cinnamon.

Mr. Quirk's eyes blinked once. They blinked again. His tongue stuck just out of his mouth, and he licked his lips.

"Take him to the hospital," Dr. Quicksolve said.

The medic twins each grabbed an arm and lifted Mr. Quirk straight up. His legs stayed tangled, and they carried him out of the room.

"What happened?" Sergeant Shurshot asked, not sure she understood what she had just witnessed.

What did happen?

Answer on page 95.

Break Time

"He just wanders off." Officer Boysenberry was explaining why he was assigned to "assist" Detective Elliott Savant. "He's really a genius, but he gets so deep into his own thoughts, he forgets what he's doing and where he is. Though, sometimes I think he's just playing."

Junior, sitting in the front seat of his dad's VW Beetle, turned back toward Boysenberry sitting alone in the back. "Sort of living in his own reality?" he asked.

"Oh, no! He would be upset if he heard you say that. No, no. He's always 'searching for the truth.' He would tell you people who 'live in their own reality' are nuts by definition. He would say it is a perception thing. 'The truth is always there to be found,' he would say," Boysenberry explained.

"I agree with him on that," Dr. Quicksolve said. He turned the car onto North Main Street.

"There he is!" Junior said. He pointed to a man with a white cane and dark glasses, obviously looking carefully both ways before crossing a side street ahead of them, tapping his cane in front of him.

"That's him, all right," Boysenberry said. "Who else would wear a trench coat and galoshes on a warm day like this?"

"Who else has that wild black hair and bushy mustache?" Junior added.

They stopped at the curb and called to Detective Savant, who pretended he didn't hear them. When Dr. Quicksolve kept driving slowly along beside him, Elliott finally gave up and climbed into the backseat next to Boysenberry. "I had you fooled," he said. He folded up the cane and put it into his pocket.

"Not for a minute," Boysenberry said.

"We've gotten news about a possible bank robbery," Dr. Quicksolve said, changing the subject.

"Oh?" Elliott said.

"There's word a crime organization from Chicago is planning a robbery here in town today," Dr. Quicksolve explained.

They went through the main part of town and continued down South Main past a small donut shop with a big sign that said "Donut Sale! This Morning Only!"

"Time for a break?" Boysenberry asked.

Dr. Quicksolve looked at his watch. "It's not really coffee time yet."

They passed another donut shop and then another.

They both had signs saying there was a sale on donuts that morning. One sign added "Southside Special."

"The trouble is we just don't know which bank they are aiming for," Dr. Quicksolve said.

When they got to the Community Bank on the southern edge of town, Dr. Quicksolve pulled over to the curb across from the bank. Here there was yet another donut shop with a sign in front that said "Special Donut Sale—This Morning Only!" A police car was parked in front of it. Another black and white police car was signaling to turn into the driveway. Junior recognized Officer Longarm and waved to him.

"Turn around!" Elliott said suddenly. "Now!"

"Good point!" Dr. Quicksolve said.

What had they decided?

Answer on page 95.

Answers

Now You See Him! Now You Don't! **(page 6)**—
Captain Rootumout was right. They wouldn't risk so
much in diamonds to balloons that couldn't be
controlled. Dr. Quicksolve thought the balloon man
should be questioned because it looked like he might
have let the balloons go as a diversion to distract the
police while his partner or partners got away.

Snowflakes and Signatures **(page 9)**—No one
writes his signature exactly the same way a second
time. Like snowflakes, they're always a little different.
A perfect match would show that one signature was a
forgery. Someone must have traced over a copy of the
first signature.

Camping Crooks **(page 12)**—Dr. Quicksolve,
always suspicious of people who pretend to be experts,
noticed the two men did not seem to be very well
prepared for camping and hiking. They were
collecting water in kitchen pans, and there was no sign
of canteens or even a simple container that would keep
bugs, leaves, and dirt out of their water.

Junior noticed the loafers—not good hiking shoes.
They both noticed the dark shirts and jeans, colors
that attract mosquitoes. The mosquito bites on the
man's neck also indicated they were unprepared.
Finally, they noticed the men wore jackets on a hot
morning, possibly to hide guns. The police were
staked out and ready late that night when the two men
approached.

Swimming Contest (page 16)—Junior figured out the girls had tricked him. He had agreed to the bet "...*we* can swim farther than you can." He realized they intended to add their distances together. He thought he could outswim either of them, but not both of them. Fauna would wait to start until Junior and Flora were done. Then she would swim just enough so her score and her sister's total combined was higher than Junior's score.

"You didn't think we were betting that we both could beat you, did you?" Flora said later.

"We is we," Fauna said.

A Cash Withdrawal (page 19)—Dr. Quicksolve wondered why the robber seemed unconcerned about the woman seeing his face when he came in and went out. He suspected the man might have tossed the bag of money into her car while the clerk was on the floor behind the counter. He wouldn't care if she saw his face because she was his partner. Dr. Quicksolve figured her description would not match the suspect's, but the bag of money in her car would prove her part in the robbery!

Seven Hills Run (page 21)—Dr. Quicksolve didn't think the robber would want to stand out and be noticed so obviously by going downhill against the flow of the racers. He figured the getaway car would be waiting up the hill on the first side street, since the main road was blocked off for the race. He had seen a runner begin to limp as if his leg hurt. That would give him a good reason for walking away from the race and going down a side street where he could escape.

Besides that, who would suspect the one person in the race who was *walking* away from the crime scene?

Strike Up the Band (page 25)—Prissy found that the doorjamb strike where the lock cylinder was supposed to go was filled with bubble gum. Junior figured out what she was talking about before she explained it because he found two bubble gum wrappers under John Bigdood's chair. He chewed the gum in class and stuck it in the doorjamb when he left class so he could come back after school and steal the instruments.

A Will and a Way (page 28)—Fred had the right idea. There was a ZIP code in 1979, but only five digits were used. It was not until 1981 that the Postal Service introduced the voluntary nine-digit ZIP code.

Campus Cop (page 30)—Dr. Quicksolve looked down at the pavement and saw two wet spots and a line of water that trailed toward the exit and another trail that went toward the boys at the other end. Even if the trail didn't reach all the way, he knew it must be from the discharge of water dripping from the air conditioner of the closed sports car. It was not likely the guys in the convertible would have their air conditioner on with the top down.

Mighty Neighborly (page 33)—If Timmy had gone outside to break the window after Jack left, Tyedye would have barked again. The break-in could easily have occurred before either neighbor was roused from sleep. In a windy storm, the rain often pelts only one side of the house and would not enter a window on the other side. This one is still a mystery.

Merger Murder (page 35)—Dr. Quicksolve figured Tom Smitt touched the ink on the paper while it was wet because he was left-handed. (Lefties often get ink on their hands because of the "upside down" way many of them hold their pens, as has been shown in other Dr. Quicksolve cases.) Dr. Quicksolve also expected to see Carl Cornet sign the paper with his right hand.

Claudia Mousepad, Carl Cornet's girlfriend and Tom Smitt's secretary, would have known that Carl was right-handed and Tom left-handed. She would have known that it was unlikely that her boyfriend would touch the ink and quite likely that Tom Smitt would, and she was ruthless enough to take the chance to put her boyfriend in charge of the new company.

Stolen Contract (page 37)—Edie just started work that day and wouldn't have known that Gail would be exercising and watching television at noon. Dr. Quicksolve suspected that Gail's secretary, Charlotte, took the contract. She would know that Gail exercised with her back toward the door and the television loud enough to be heard over the noise of the treadmill. Charlotte would have known that this noise would have prevented Gail from hearing her come in and steal the contract.

Winter Break (page 39)—Dr. Quicksolve did not believe the suspect's story about someone running down a hill on a slippery side street. He wanted a record of the scene, including the slippery street, the hill, and, as far as he could tell, no indication of footprints in the snow leading from the street into someone's yard. Turning around so it looks like you are not running away is a good trick, but it did not work this time.

Sayahh.com (page 42)—Dr. Quicksolve knew the tools Paul had were exactly what he would need to take the pins out of the door hinges while Mr. Flemm was in his office. After he took out the metal pins and replaced them temporarily with straws, he waited until Julie left the building and simply pushed the door open, breaking the straws. He would simply replace the metal pins and lock the door when he left with the loot.

Cookie Jar Caper (page 45)—Dr. Quicksolve thought the suspect from Mexico had a pretty good alibi if he had relatives in the neighborhood. He could have easily been on the wrong street. He would have been foolish to rob a house in a strange neighborhood when he could not have had time to learn about the situation—if anyone was home or how long they would be gone. He had no way of knowing about the money. He could not have seen a "slightly open" window from the street, and he hardly had time to go around checking the ground-level windows to find them all locked. He also would more likely have broken open the door from the garage to the house where he had some cover rather than being so obvious by using a ladder out in the yard.

Dr. Quicksolve actually thought Miss Stretchitout

was a better suspect. She knew about the money in the cookie jar. She knew exactly when Mrs. Resident would be gone. She could probably see the open window through her upstairs window. She certainly was athletic enough to handle the aluminum ladder that she knew was in the garage. She could have pushed her hair up under her cap and let her shirttails down to look like Mr. Resident painting the house when she carried the ladder around and climbed up to the window. She probably saw the strange car and took down the license number to look innocent and helpful and throw the suspicion onto someone else.

Kidnapped Kicker (page 49)—Dr. Quicksolve suspected Worthless staged the whole incident to get some money from his parents. Professional kidnappers would not risk getting caught for kidnapping a teenager with bodyguards around for only $10,000. Also, they would have no way of knowing Worthless was going to run into the brush just at that time.

Dr. Quicksolve was surprised he ran to get the ball in the first place. If he shot the ball over the goal and it went out of bounds, it would come back into the game in the possession of the other team. The goalie or a defender usually chases after it. It is very unlikely that an offensive player would retrieve the ball for the other team. Also, Worthless, who was old enough to drive, could have easily had some kind of vehicle hidden for him to drive away.

Another Warehouse Murder (page 52)—Dr. Quicksolve has noted the drops of blood by the safe, quite a distance from where the owner was shot dead.

The blood indicates the crook hurt himself with the hammer and chisel trying to open the safe. One of the officers should have noticed an injured hand when he handcuffed his man. If one officer said his man was not injured, it would have to be the other, assuming the criminal was one of the two suspects. Beekerjar will know for certain after tests are done on the blood.

Following Cecil Sapp (page 55)—The suspicious behavior, of course, was that the man had entered the bank and spotted Cecil before he went out and showed up at Cecil's drive-thru window. Also, Dr. Quicksolve noticed the check had a relatively low number of 118. Ninety percent of bad or "hot" checks have low numbers (100–200). They are not well-established accounts. Also, frequently con men use deposit slips to cheat banks. A bad check may seem to be worth more than what is being taken out in the "less cash" column, and cash in the account makes it look like the withdrawal is covered. Deposit slips are easy to copy, and people, unfortunately, use them to write notes and things like grocery lists, etc., not realizing how easy they are to duplicate in copy machines!

Callahan and Callahan (page 59)—If the office wasn't cleaned after the kidnapping, it will have a lot of fibers from Casey's red sweater where he was dragged across the floor. Likewise, the fibers will be in the motel room.

Mystery Train (page 63)—Dr. Quicksolve said, "The angle of the shot, though it is a good thought, does not tell us much because a typical birdcage hangs on a swivel that might turn the bird and cage at various angles toward the ladies. Who owned the gun would be important, except that since they lived together, they both had access to the gun. Motive seemed to be equal, though, of course, it should be looked at. But Officer Beekerjar may have an advantage because he is a police science lab expert. He knows you can test the ladies' hands for residue samples that will tell you who has recently fired a gun. He is the one who has the best idea."

Mystery Train Two (page 67)—They both think Junior has the best idea. Everyone looked suspicious wandering around through the secret tunnels with some strange implement in his or her hands. They all may have intended to steal the candy bar. Who really did it, however, can probably best be determined by examining the wooden box that was broken into. Each tool would leave a particular kind of mark on the wood. That is how they could tell who did it!

Defining Moment (page 73)—The obvious question was why, with all those law officers who were probably armed, no one tried to stop the culprits or even seemed to be worried about chasing them.

The answer: Everyone slowly raised his or her cell phone. They all had carefully dialed 911 and let the authorities hear what was happening as they asked questions, stalling the robbers and giving information about exactly what was going on to the police on the other end of the lines. Did you notice? Sergeant Shurshot announced a robbery was taking place. Dr. Quicksolve indicated there were two men with guns.

Fred Fraudstop gave their location. Dr. Quicksolve even slowed them down a bit by offering to give them more money.

The police were waiting for them when they got off the train.

The Meditators' Incident (page 81)—Dr. Quicksolve realized that Detective Savant had gone into the kitchen to make toast, not for a snack, but to solve the problem. He figured a starving man would react to the smell of cinnamon toast and peanut butter. He was right!

Officer Boysenberry, who had the job of keeping track of the absent-minded Detective Elliott Savant, came back into the room from the kitchen and grabbed the radio from Sergeant Shurshot's belt. "Headquarters! Headquarters!" he shouted into the device. "Detective Savant has walked off again! Man at large! Man at large!"

Break Time (page 84)—Elliott and Dr. Quicksolve realized the donut sales that morning were all on the south side of town. It was quite possibly a ploy by the Chicago gang to draw all the police cars on duty to the south side so they could rob a bank on the north side of town!

Index

Answer pages are in italics.

Another Warehouse Murder, 52, *92–93*

Break Time, 84, *95*

Callahan and Callahan, 59, *93*

Camping Crooks, 12, *87*

Campus Cop, 30, *89*

Cash Withdrawal, A, 19, *88*

Cookie Jar Caper, 45, *91–92*

Defining Moment, 73, *94–95*

Dr. J. L. Quicksolve, 5

Elliott Savant, 78,

Following Cecil Sapp, 55, *93*

Kidnapped Kicker, 49, *92*

Meditators' Incident, The, 81, *95*

Merger Murder, 35, *90*

Mighty Neighborly, 33, *89–90*

Mystery Train, 63, *93–94*

Mystery Train Two, 67, *94*

Now You See Him! Now You Don't!, 6, *87*

Sayahh.com, 42, *91*

Seven Hills Run, 21, *88–89*

Snowflakes and Signatures, 9, *87*

Stolen Contract, 37, *90*

Strike Up the Band, 25, *89*

Swimming Contest, 16, *88*

Will and a Way, A, 28, *89*

Winter Break, 39, *90–91*